D1504631

# Strategies for Attracting Good Luck

* Cash In On the Luck Of Others
* Mystical Secrets of Good Luck
* Techniques to Attract Good Luck
* Find Your Own Good Luck Within
* The Power of Luck Confirmed
* Cash In On Your Lucky Cycles

# Gail Howard

# You *Can* Make Luck Happen

My Smart Luck® lottery strategies will improve your win probability, but to capture the top prize worth millions and beat those astronomical odds, you need to attract some good old-fashioned LUCK! Yes, there are strategies even for attracting luck. This book shows you how to cash in by optimizing your good luck. You can't afford to leave your luck to chance!

## CASH IN ON THE LUCK OF OTHERS

When you form a lottery pool or syndicate (group play) and share the ticket cost – and the winnings – with others, your group is also pooling its luck. A jackpot could be won because of the luck just one of the members brings to your pool – or because of the combined luck of all the members.

Select your partners carefully when deciding whom you want to include in your group. Share your luck with *winners*, not with losers. You want to enhance your own luck, not dilute its strength by burdening the group's energy with losers.

Avoid negative people who always see the glass half empty. Not only are they unlucky, but they dampen enthusiasm and drain energy from others. One quick way to tell the winners from the losers? Simply ask them! "Do you think you are a lucky person?"

Many people quickly admit, "I'm unlucky. I never win anything," — and they usually don't. They won't bring any more luck to your group than they bring to themselves. So, by inviting only upbeat, cheerful, happy people to join your pool, you could cash in on the luck of others.

Unlike Lotto numbers that are randomly drawn, good luck is not randomly distributed. If it were, we would all be equally lucky. But you know that is not the case. Some people are obviously luckier than others.

If you study the characteristics of people who seem to be "born lucky," you will see that they have certain distinctive traits. Look for these traits in people you include in your lottery pool or syndicate for group play. And increase your luck quotient by cultivating these traits in yourself.

Lucky people are outgoing, optimistic and always look for a positive result or outcome.

Lucky people don't wait for good things to happen; they *make* them happen. In luck, patience is not a virtue.

Lucky people are not afraid to take calculated risks and are willing to accept small losses without anxiety or fear.

Lucky people choose their own destiny. They are in control or their lives and take responsibility for their actions and decisions.

Lucky people never give up, unless they see they are on the wrong track, in which case they quickly cut their losses.

Lucky people are prepared so that when an opportunity presents itself, they are ready to take advantage of it.

Lucky people are compassionate and have a generous spirit. They are giving, not only of material possessions, but with their time, energy and love as well.

Lucky people want the best for others and bear no envy or malice.

Lucky people listen to their intuition, the subconscious all-knowing self that resides inside each one of us. That inner self knows what is best for us and will help us if we know how to listen.

Lucky people have goals. They know what they want and work toward achieving their goals. It is true that "God helps those who help themselves."

## MYSTICAL SECRETS OF GOOD LUCK

No one should play games of chance out of desperation because they need the winnings. The needy have a greater fear of losing the hard-earned money they gamble with. It is just one of life's dirty tricks that the very fear of losing blocks the winning forces. Let me explain how the power of the mind influences your good or bad luck, according to ancient metaphysical teachings.

Thoughts are charged with energy, especially when triggered by emotion. A negative thought attracts a negative response. Fear attracts exactly that which one fears. On the other hand, a strong desire for a particular goal that is charged with positive energy, attracts a positive response— especially when every effort is made to attain that goal.

Thoughts are actually *things* with shape and form, which have been seen by clairvoyants gifted with astral vision. To illustrate my point, have you ever "lost" a thought when you walked into another room, only to reconnect with that thought when you returned to the room where the thought had first occurred to you? You were able to "remember" because the thought form was still intact in the room where it had originated.

When a thought form is not reinforced, it soon dissipates. But a thought that is constantly energized by repetition gradually takes on a power of its own. Therefore, if you have it in your mind (or even 'joke' about it with others) that you are unlucky or a loser, you assuredly will be. To be a winner, you must think of yourself as a winner.

## TECHNIQUES TO ATTRACT GOOD LUCK

To be lucky, you must start to think of yourself as a lucky person. Think this positive thought several times a day. The more you energize a thought form, the stronger and more powerful it will become. Your winnings will increase along with your good luck — not only in the lottery, but in other aspects of your life as well.

Also, it is important to wish well for others. Your good thoughts for the welfare of others comes back to you like a boomerang. If you wish others harm, this also boomerangs back to you. When you truly believe you are lucky and you radiate love for others and work hard to make your goals a reality, everything falls into place easily. I know this to be true because it has worked for me and I AM VERY LUCKY!!!

Winning a lottery jackpot would be wonderful, but it is family, friends and loving people in our lives who bring us the greatest joy. And for that, we should give thanks for our good fortune. No one who has friends or loved ones can consider himself unlucky. Those who say, "I'm unlucky. I never win anything," should realize that they have won the most important prize of all — the love of family and friends.

If you have such love, you are truly a winner. And you can use that mental image of being a winner to help you in other areas of your life. If you can feel like a winner — it doesn't matter whether it's in love, friendship, health, business or the lottery — you can attract more of the winning forces to yourself.

Treat lightly the losses or disappointments that come into your life. Deal with them but don't dwell on them. Let the negative influences be fleeting experiences. You don't want your subconscious to pick up negative patterns. Your mental energy should be channeled in a positive way.

In your mind you have the power to make your thoughts a reality. If you can truly believe you are a winner, you will reinforce the winning patterns in your life. If certain experiences in the past have left you bitter or negative, try to forgive others, or even yourself, and let go of negative past experiences that have left you feeling unlucky. Neutralize those negative thoughts and convert that energy to success.

Start loving yourself more. If you write a list of all your good qualities, you will see that you are a person who deserves love and all the wonderful things life has to offer. Many people are losers because subconsciously they feel they don't deserve to have good things happen to them.

Be less critical and give yourself a pat on the back whenever possible. Extend this love and appreciation to others as well. Try giving a compliment when you feel like criticizing. See what happens. You might be surprised. The positive reaction of others reinforces your own sense of well-being.

Approach life with enthusiasm and optimism. Expect the best to happen for you. The saying goes, "As a man sees his own face reflected in a placid pool, so life frowns or smiles on him, depending on the way he first looks at it."

People who are naturally optimistic and enthusiastic usually are so because their past experience in attracting luck has been positive. Have you noticed how luck seems to surround people who have a healthy, cheerful, positive outlook on life?

Why not make a deliberate effort to improve your luck with a winning image of yourself. If you put your mind to it, you can make positive changes that will last a lifetime. Take stock of yourself and think about the changes you'd like to make.

Set short and long term goals for yourself. Think about what you want to accomplish this year, the next two, three or five years, or even farther out. It's always good to have a plan, an attainable goal just slightly out of reach.

And, of course, you should also have wishes and dreams that you hope one day will become reality. People who don't map out a life and plan the direction they want it to take, usually drift aimlessly or get stuck in a rut.

## FIND YOUR OWN GOOD LUCK WITHIN

Go to a quiet spot where you can be completely alone for several minutes. Bring a pen and pad of paper with you. Relax your mind by taking three long deep breaths. Close your eyes. Breathe in slowly through your nose until your lungs are full, hold it a few moments, then release the air very slowly though your lips. Do this slowly three times.

Now that your mind is clear and relaxed, ask yourself how the ideal disciplined you would live your life. Don't think about it. Let your mind be an empty vessel that catches superior intelligence from your unconscious levels.

As the thoughts come tumbling out, write them down. Don't judge, question or censor thoughts as they come to you. Don't write complete sentences now. Just capture the thoughts on paper. You can organize them neatly later.

Ask your inner self where you want to be a year from now, five years from now, ten years from now. Then wait quietly for the answers. Only YOU can make changes happen in your life.

Ask your unconscious to examine all areas of your life—your self-image, your work, health, relationships with others, etc. Concentrate on one specific area at a time. Write down the thoughts as they come to you. Later when you read your notes, you'll be astonished at the inspired thoughts you received from your inner conscious levels. Do this as often as you want. You'll get better at it each time you do it.

Don't be afraid to dream big dreams—let your mind soar. Then plan, step by step, how you would go about achieving that goal. Put one foot in front of the other on your path toward making your dream a reality. If this means hard work or gathering more knowledge, then do it. Do what you have to do to work toward your goal. You may be amazed at what you can accomplish!

You must believe in yourself. Know that you can do anything you set your mind to do. Don't listen to others who tell you it can't be done. Luck comes with forging ahead and taking risks when you believe in yourself.

Only those who run the risk of possible failure can achieve success. You can't win a lottery if you don't buy a ticket. However, you can minimize the risk by being prepared for the goal you want to achieve. When you are prepared, you can take advantage of "being in the right place at the right time." Planning, preparation and confidence increase your luck immeasurably. Be ready for opportunity when it comes knocking on your door. As golfer Lee Travino once said, "The harder I work, the luckier I get."

Don't look for approval from others. Give yourself credit for each small success along the path toward your goal. You must earn your own self-respect — which is a reflection of your self-esteem. The more you do, the more you'll be able to do.

Once your sub-conscious knows you are a winner, there will be no limit to what you are capable of accomplishing. The two most important ingredients are a strong emotional desire for the goal and a willingness to work hard to make your goal a reality. You can apply this to everything in life — your work, your love life, your relations with friends and family, your health, even to games of chance.

## THE POWER OF LUCK CONFIRMED

People who *consistently* win lottery prizes, invest time and effort in selecting their numbers. It's comforting to think that to win the lottery jackpot, all you need is a buck and a little bit of luck. But, jackpot-winning luck is out of the realm of mathematical probability. It happens only to that one in millions. Luck is an added plus that you can't really count on until it happens to you.

On May 31, 1986, I got lucky using my systems and I beat odds of one in 48,696 to win a second prize in New York's Lotto 6/48. I had five numbers on one line – and the sixth winning number was in its place on the second line! In addition, I won a third prize, beating the odds of one in 950.

On the same day in the same New York Lotto game, Sharon Jaynes used my system and beat the odds of one in 12,271,512 to win the first prize jackpot. Sharon Jaynes won $13.8 million and I won $1,187. We both used my system and we both got lucky, but that day, Sharon Jaynes was financially luckier than I was.

Mrs. Jaynes arrived at her press conference waving my book, which she kept in front of her during the interview. This generous-spirited woman proclaimed to the media that she had used Gail Howard's book to win her jackpot and said she would stop playing the lottery "to give someone else a chance to win."

Newspapers across the country carried the Associated Press article in which Sharon Jaynes credited my book for her 13.8 million dollar jackpot win. The wonderful publicity resulting from her genuine heartfelt gratitude meant more to me than winning the jackpot.

It certainly helps to focus your desires. I'll let you in on a little secret. Many of my jackpot winners "knew" in their hearts without a doubt that they were going to win the jackpot. They had unwavering faith that with my systems it was going to happen…and, for them, it did!!

Mitch Drummond was so certain he was going to win a jackpot with my systems that he consulted tax and financial advisors so he would be prepared when he finally struck it rich.

In his letter to me, Mitch wrote: "I knew that your system would work. I just had to give it time. Gail, I had so much confidence in your system that I terminated military service after 14.9 years. It was only 5.3 till retirement. I did not have a job lined up.

"But 45 minutes before the balls were drawn, I had a feeling come over me, Gail, that could have only been from God and it told me to play. In 45 minutes I selected the numbers, placed them in the wheel and got them to the store. Forty-five minutes later I was practically a half-million dollars richer."

Will and Juanita Richey combined my system with their own positive mental attitudes to win a Michigan Lotto jackpot of $1,190,932. Juanita said, "I made a decision to win the Michigan Lotto within a short period of time. We started planning as if we had already won it. Once we got Gail Howard's book, I realized that it was the way we were going to do it. We were totally committed to winning that jackpot and it happened."

Juanita advises people who want to win a big lotto jackpot to decide that they really want to win and then to be committed and really serious about it. "Have some specific goals in mind of what you want to do with your money and then go at it wholeheartedly."

Will said, "Before I won the lotto jackpot, I was already a millionaire. I just hadn't collected my money."

Active church goers, the Richeys had committed to a three-year, $12,000 building-fund donation without knowing where they would get the money. "We went ahead with our plans and acted as if the money was already there. We just knew the money would come and it did." Will added, "Some people want a lot of things but they never take time to read the instruction book."

There seemed no way out of Janice and Lonnis Eavey's mounting burden of debt except to win the lottery. In spite of financial woes, Lonnis found inner strength in his faith that he would win the lottery. On February 25, 1995, Lonnis had a hunch that tonight was it.

Janice wrote, "We decided to sell our car as we couldn't afford the insurance anymore. We sold it to my nephew for $150. Lonnis asked me if he could bet $42 to play your 18-number system.

"Two days later, our brother-in-law asked, 'Did you get your lotto tickets?' Lonnis replied, 'Yes we did and we got the winning ticket!!' It was like Lonnis knew he was holding the winning ticket.
"We are doing our best to use our money wisely and would like to thank you for your system. IT REALLY WORKS!! Sincerely, Lonnis M. & Janice M. Eavey"

The Eavey's were one of three winners who split Michigan's $45,851,401 jackpot on February 25, 1995. Their share was $15,283,800.

The faith of those three jackpot winners was unwavering and, for them, it worked. Have the same positive attitude, but PLEASE, DO NOT SPEND MORE THAN YOU CAN AFFORD on tickets!!

## CASH IN ON YOUR LUCKY CYCLES

Luck does come in streaks. If you are on a losing streak, cut back on the amount you spend on tickets. When you start winning you can afford to spend more because you may be on a roll! – and because you are playing with "their" money.

Although my scientific systems for picking winning lotto combinations are based on mathematical probability, I think luck cycles can be used to maximize your lottery budget. By knowing when your luck is running high or low, you can budget your playing dollars accordingly.

Kenneth Dickkerson, author of the book, *How to Win Games of Chance* (published by Ballantine Books), researched this method by plotting the winning cycles of many winners, including myself and several jackpot winners. The results were so conclusive that Ken limits his own lottery play to the times when he thinks his luck cycles are the most favorable.

I was astonished when Ken analyzed my year's collection of winning Lotto tickets and found that 53 percent of my wins occurred during my luckiest cycle, and only 4 percent of my wins occurred during my least lucky cycle.

This is how it works. Find your astrological Sun Sign that corresponds to the date you were born. Next to it is the element your sign represents. For example, if you were born on April 5th, your sun sign is Aries and your element is fire.

If, for example, your element is fire, the luckiest times to play games of chance would be when the sun is in any of the fire signs, such as Aries (March 21st to April 19th), Leo (July 23rd to August 22nd) or Sagittarius (November 22nd to December 21st). Your next luckiest time to play would be when the sun is in any of the air signs, such as Gemini, Libra or Aquarius.

| SUN SIGN | From | To | ELEMEN |
|---|---|---|---|
| ARIES | March 21st | April 19th | FIRE |
| TAURUS | April 20th | May 20th | EARTH |
| GEMINI | May 21st | June 20th | AIR |
| CANCER | June 21st | July 22nd | WATERR |
| LEO | July 23rd | August 22nd | FIRE |
| VIRGO | August 23rd | Sept. 22nd | EARTH |
| LIBRA | September 23rd | October 22nd | AIR |
| SCORPIO | October 23rd | November 21st | WATER |
| SAGITTARIUS | November 22nd | December 21st | FIRE |
| CAPRICORN | December 22nd | January 19th | EARTH |
| AQUARIUS | January 20th | February 18th | AIR |
| PISCES | February 19th | March 20th | WATER |

If your element is fire, you would still be somewhat (but not as) lucky when the sun is in the earth signs of

Taurus, Virgo or Capricorn. (You may then want to reduce the amount you spend on Lotto tickets.) As a fire sign, you would have the least luck when the sun is in the water signs of Cancer, Scorpio or Pisces. At those times, you may decide not to play at all.

Listed below are the luck ratings for each of the elements. You may want to consider the elements of the sun signs of the partners in your Lotto pool as well!

| ELEMENTS | Luckiest | Next Luckiest | Somewhat Lucky | Least Lucky |
|---|---|---|---|---|
| FIRE | Fire | Air | Earth | Water |
| AIR | Air | Fire | Water | Earth |
| EARTH | Earth | Water | Fire | Air |
| WATER | Water | Earth | Air | Fire |

When Kenneth Dickkerson analyzed the 72 times I had won lottery prizes in one year, I was amazed at the results. I was born in July. My sun sign is Cancer and my element is water. Here is the breakdown according to the number of prizes I won when the sun was in each element.

WATER - 38 Prizes (53%)
EARTH - 17 Prizes (24%)
AIR - 14 Prizes (19%)
FIRE - 3 Prizes ( 4%)

I highly recommend Ken Dickkerson's book, *How to Win Games of Chance*, which tells you how to discover your lucky numbers and lucky cycles to win at lotteries, bingo, sweepstakes, casino gambling and the racetrack. You'll find the sun sign and elements timing method on pages 23 to 28 in his 260-page book.

Two first prize jackpot winners used my systems and Ken's timing to hit it big. For information about his products and services, or to buy the book directly from Ken, write to: Kenneth Dickkerson, The PTN, P.O. Box 7893, Chandler, Arizona 85246-7893. Visit his web site at: www.dickkerson2win.com.

Explore your personal key numbers and learn all about yourself in Lloyd Strayhorn's book, *Numbers and You* published by Ballantine Books. Strayhorn has appeared on Oprah Winfrey, Regis and Kathy Lee, Geraldo Rivera and Montiel Williams shows. His interview with Katie Couric on Eye to Eye can be seen on YouTube.com on the Internet. For information about his numerology and astrology services, write to: Lloyd Strayhorn, 2266 5th Ave., Box 136, New York, NY 10037. Visit his web site at: www.numbersand you.com.

Another book I recommend is Lynne Palmer's *Money Magic*, published by Star Bright Publishers. In *Money Magic*, Lynne explains what attracts wealth according to your sun sign; how to overcome obstacles in making money; relationships that can make you gain or lose money, and much more.

Lynne Palmer is the author of forty books, including the famous *Astrological Almanac*, which is published annually. It gives the best dates for 500 categories of activities and is a unique approach to planning your life. If you want to know what is in store for your future, I highly recommend Lynne Palmer's 2-Year Future Forecast based on your exact time of birth. For information about her books and personal horoscope services, write to: Lynne Palmer, 850 East Desert Inn Road, Suite 912, Las Vegas, NV 89109, or visit her web site: www.lynnepalmer.com.

And be sure to visit my website at www.smartluck.com to see my lottery books and software and to use my free lottery tips and free wheels that have already won jackpots.

## WHAT IT'S LIKE TO BE A JACKPOT WINNER

Winning the lottery is a blessing to more than 99 percent of jackpot winners. It brings joy to the winner and to his family. Life becomes easier. Worries about paying bills and credit card debts vanish. In many cases, the winner is freed from having to earn a living, and can pursue a life-long dream in another area of endeavor.

A really big winner can quit his job and have free time to fulfill a dream: travel the world, start a business, write a book, become a philanthropist or become a political power to be reckoned with if the win is large enough.

The news media are interested in publicizing only the winners who mess up. Seldom will you read stories about happy jackpot winners whose lives are changed for the better. The media are generally against the lottery so the only stories that interest them are those they can dig up about lottery winners who get into trouble after the big win. They look for the story of "man bites dog" not the more common "dog bites man."

After I appeared on the ABC television show, *Good Morning America*, I became the unofficial contact for the media looking for lottery stories. Every reporter or producer who contacted me asked the same question: "Do you know of any winner whose life was ruined because he or she won the lottery?"

A winner whose life was ruined because he won the lottery was a loser before he won. If he hadn't won the lottery, the loser would find something or someone else to blame on for his poor character or his misery.

A person who is extremely careless and extravagant could not only go broke, but end up with massive debts. This is a rare occurrence because most big winners are level headed after the win, just as they were before.

One's tendencies before a big lottery win are the same or intensified after the win. A person who was irresponsible with his money before winning a lottery jackpot will not change when he has more money to be responsible for. If a jackpot winner commits murder, don't tell me, "The lottery win made him do it." I won't buy it.

I have had the opportunity to talk personally with each of the first prize jackpot winners who used my Smart Luck systems to win – and other jackpot winners as well. I asked them all how the win affected them and how it changed their lives. Their answers were so uniformly similar that a composite profile would best describe the typical winner.

When you win "the big one," this may be YOUR experience as well.

When the winner checks his ticket and sees that he has all the winning numbers, he never believes it. He checks and rechecks and checks again. Even when friends or family confirm the ticket is a winner, he still refuses to believe it. He feels no reaction, just disbelief. Most likely he is in a state of shock.

When finally he is convinced that he really has won, he feels a mounting excitement. His heart starts pounding, breathing becomes rapid and he is infused with energy. Adrenaline pours into his system and he can't sit still. He feels agitated but elated. Some feel their knees shaking, some shake all over. Some break out in a sweat. Some winners jump up and down, screaming.

Wilbert M. won $5.3 million with my system. When he realized he hit the jackpot, Will told me, "I screamed and cried at the same time. I felt scared, but very excited, bewildered, weak, nervous, shocked . . . I ran around the lunch room table like a caged rat and fell down on my knees crying."

With very few exceptions, most big winners claim they were terribly excited – even high. The few who said they accepted the win calmly, claimed they "knew" they were going to win.

In most cases, the winner can't sleep all night. His mind races, trying to fathom what it all means and what impact the win will have on his life. How will he spend it, how will he invest it, should he retire early or keep on working. Thoughts race through his mind. He fantasizes about all the things he has wanted and now will be able to afford. He can be a hero helping family, friends and neighbors in need.

The winner feels an uncontrollable urge to tell someone, to shout out to the world, that he has just won the lottery jackpot. If he had to keep it bottled up inside, he feels he would burst. One man was in the hospital when he discovered he had just won a million-dollar jackpot. He screamed to the patient in the other bed that he had just become a millionaire. His  roommate was in a coma.

Many winners don't fully realize they have won until they file the claim with the lottery office. One winner told me, "I was in a taxi on my way home after filing my claim, when suddenly I was struck by the reality of my win." Her voice abruptly pierced the stillness as she shrieked, "I just won a million dollars!!" The taxi driver thought she was mentally deranged.

After news of the win leaks out, the telephone rings non-stop for a period of two weeks to a month. The calls from friends and well-wishers congratulating the winner are welcome because  winners want to share their happy news with the world. One winner told me he had an insatiable urge to shake hands with everyone after his win. The larger the win – and the more publicized it is – the sooner the jackpot winner finds it necessary to disconnect his phone and get an unlisted number...or even get out of town.

Everyone loves a winner! His good fortune captures the public's imagination and gives hope to others. The winner receives many warm congratulatory wishes from strangers as well as from friends. A new lottery millionaire family, upon returning home from their first press conference, found a parade awaiting them and a block party going on. A hastily erected neon sign on their front lawn welcomed them home. Said Mrs. T., "The town went wild. Everybody was so happy for us." The mayor of the small, depressed town in upstate New York told them it was a great morale booster for the community.

The downside of a lottery win is that friends, relatives, neighbors, and even strangers think now that you are flush with money they should have a share of this manna from heaven. But even worse are the financial "experts" who want to invest your money and "make you rich."

The main targets for donations and requests for money are the larger jackpot winners. Mail is often sent to them in care of the state lottery office. Unless the winner requests that this mail be forwarded to him, it is returned to the sender with a polite note. Much of the mail is sent to congratulate the winner.

Some write in hope that the winner's luck will rub off on them. Some are just looking for pen pals. Most of the letters requesting donations or money come from overseas – especially from Southeast Asia and India. Many of the letters from the Philippines are from people asking the winner to adopt them – and their families! The writer usually promises to work hard for the mega-bucks winner.

One $3 million winner received a letter from a convict in prison in the Philippines. He needed to have an operation on his ulcer. He said the prison would release him if the winner agreed to bring him to the USA and permit him to work for her as a chauffeur/gardener. He was doing time for murder.

Winners of small cash-5 jackpots are also tapped for loans or gifts of money by friends or relatives. The most important word any jackpot winner can learn to say is an emphatic "No!" Many jackpot winners have gone bankrupt because they allowed leechy friends and relatives to bleed them dry. If a friendship is lost because the winner fails to cave in to greedy demands, it was not a true friendship anyway. It is when you are down and out or when you come into a sudden windfall that you find out who your true friends are. A real friend is happy for you and expects nothing from you.

Most winners keep their jobs, except for those who were not happy with them anyway or were near retirement. Some of the more enterprising go into business for themselves, doing work very similar to that which they had been doing before they won their jackpot.

Nearly everyone identifies through his work. Work fulfills and sustains us and we are reluctant to give that up. Also, our co-workers, clients or customers fill a social need for the major part of the day. After traveling a bit and fixing up everything there is to fix around the house, most winners look for a job or a business to run.

How do co-workers treat a millionaire winner when he comes back to work? In most cases he is heartily congratulated and then it's back to work as usual. But when a millionaire winner returns to a low-skilled job, co-workers chide him for continuing to work and depriving someone else of a job who needs the money. Often there is envy, or a supervisor who feels threatened.

Winners of very large jackpots have complained to me that life-long friends defer to them now that they are rich. Winners tell me they haven't changed, but some of their friends hold them in awe and can't be natural around them anymore. Winners miss the old camaraderie they had with their friends before they won.

At a lottery millionaires' party I attended, I didn't see flashy or expensive jewelry. If jewelry and flash were not a part of their lives before, they are not, in most cases, after the win. Except for upgrading their houses or buying a new car, most of the winners retain their former lifestyles. Some move into a larger house – but usually not far from the old neighborhood.

One recent jackpot winner told me, "I'm not sure I want my life to change. It's a little scary." Also, it is difficult to change a lifetime of habit. The wife of one megabucks winner confessed somewhat sheepishly that she still uses coupons and shops for bargains in the supermarket – even though her husband reminds her that they cannot possibly spend all the money they have in a lifetime.

One of the unexpected benefits of a jackpot win is a new sense of self-esteem. A lottery winner develops more confidence and a feeling of self-worth. He gains respect for himself and feels more in control of his life. And he becomes more gregarious.

Even the facial expression seems to change. This before-and-after-the-win comparison was obvious when viewing videos made on the day the winners claimed their jackpots, which were shown at one millionaires' party. They all looked much younger now – and most attributed it to the peace of mind that comes with lack of financial strain and worry. So another side-benefit of a lotto  jackpot win seems to be an element of rejuvenation!

Many winners told me they were burdened with debt before they won. One $3 million winner confided that he owed $40,000 on his credit cards prior to his win, and that he was "near the brink," considering suicide.

For most winners, a jackpot win spells security and freedom from worry about bills. It also opens opportunity that didn't exist before. It is still a dream to winners I spoke with – no matter how many years ago they had won. Even though they are busily spending the windfall, they can't quite believe it really had happened to them. The question often voiced was, "Why me? ... Why me?"

It appears that people are much more grateful when they win a large sum of money than when they earn it. One man who had severe financial problems before his jackpot win expressed it to me this way: "I would kiss the rear end of a donkey for the New York State Lottery!"

The day after the party, one of the millionaires told me that she had never been to a party where everyone was so joyous. Some say money cannot buy happiness, but who knows, maybe it can!

I sincerely hope that you, too, one day will experience the joy of winning the Big One. But keep in mind the odds to beat are very steep. For that reason you must decide on a budget you feel comfortable with and consider lottery tickets an entertainment expense.

When you buy theater, ball game or concert tickets, you know you can afford them and you expect to have a good time. When you buy lottery tickets with the same positive attitude, negative emotions won't block the winning forces. It is one of life's dirty tricks that a fear of losing blocks the winning forces. So, never spend more money on lottery tickets than you can afford to lose. My systems reduce the odds, but no lottery system can eliminate the odds entirely.

Although more than one hundred first prize lotto jackpots have been won with my systems and strategies, most people using my systems have NOT yet won a top prize. On the other hand, Nancy and Ralph C. used my system 3014 and won $244,114 in the Florida Fantasy 5 "on the first try."

Whether you win the top prize sooner or later or never, it is important to use systems and strategies that improve your odds of winning. There are two distinct methods to help you win: Number Selection and Wheeling Systems. They can be used separately or together.

**Here are some links to FREE helpful information:**

Three Methods to Win at Lotto:
http://www.smartluck.com/3-winning-lotto-methods.htm
The All-Important Balanced Game:
http://www.smartluck.com/gail-howard-balanced-game.htm
Lottery Wheeling Explained:
http://www.smartluck.com/lotterywheeling.htm
 Why Balanced Wheels Produce So Many Jackpot Winners
http://www.smartluck.com/lotto-balanced-wheels.htm
Free Lotto Jackpot Winning Wheeling Systems:
http://www.smartluck.com/free-lotto-wheels.htm
Get the 70% lottery advantage for the lotto game you play:
http://www.smartluck.com/bestsums.htm
Free Winning Lottery Strategies and free tips for YOUR
favorite lotto game:  Click: "Choose YOUR Lotto Game
Now"  to see free tips for any lotto game in the world.
 http://www.smartluck.com/free-lottery-strategies.htm


My *Lottery Master Guide* book and Advantage software
show you how to scientifically CHOOSE your lotto
numbers. My other books and software contain
wheeling systems.  To see a description of my lottery
books and software, click:

 http://www.smartluck.com/products.htm

My best tip: Play the Cash 5 games for an easier jackpot
Win.  GOOD LUCK WITH SMART LUCK!!!

Made in the USA
San Bernardino, CA
15 October 2014